KILLER CREATURES

Claire Llewellyn

KINGFISHER

KINGFISHER

First published 2008 by Kingfisher
This edition published 2015 by Kingfisher
an imprint of Macmillan Children's Books
20 New Wharf Road, London N1 9RR
Associated companies throughout the world
www.panmacmillan.com

Consultant: David Burnie

Illustrations by Steve Weston (represented by Linden Artists)
with additional artwork by Peter Bull Studio and Lee Gibbons

ISBN 978-0-7534-3980-7

9 8 7 6 5 4 3 2 1
1TR/0815/WKT/SG(UG)/128MA

A CIP catalogue record for this book is available from the British Library.

Printed in China

Note to readers: The website addresses listed in this book are correct at the time of publishing.
However, due to the ever-changing nature of the internet, website addresses and content can change.
Websites can contain links that are unsuitable for children. The publisher cannot be held responsible
for changes in website addresses or content, or for information obtained through third-party websites.
We strongly advise that internet searches should be supervised by an adult.

The publisher would like to thank the following for permission to reproduce their images.
(t = top, b = bottom, c = centre, r = right, l = left)

Front Cover c Getty/Taxi; Pages 4lc Getty/Gallo Images-Londolozi Productions; 4-5 Seapics/Kike Calvo; 5tl Natural History Picture Agency (NHPA)/ Rich Kirchner; 5tr Frank
Lane Picture Agency (FLPA)/Minden Pictures; 5rc Corbis/Reuters; 5br Corbis/Joe McDonald; 6lc NHPA; 6-7 NHPA/Photoshot; 7t Getty/Gallo Images-Londolozi Productions;
7c NHPA/Daryl Balfour; 7bl Nature PL/Martin Dohrn; 7br Getty/Steve Bloom; 8c FLPA/Minden Pictures; 8b Nature PL/David Welling; 8br Corbis/Jeff Vanuga; 9tl Getty/
Eastcott Momatiuk; 9tr Corbis/Jeff Vanuga; 9bl NHPA/Rich Kirchner; 9br Nature PL/Larry Michael; 10tr Science Photo Library (SPL)/ Andrew Syred; 10bl Seapics/Innerspace
Visions; 11tc Corbis/Arthur Morris; 11cc Corbis/ Terry W. Eggers; 11t Getty/Fuse; 11b Alamy/Steven Kazlowski; 12tl Nature PL/Tony Heald: 12r Photolibrary/Richard
Packwood; 13t Nature PL/Christophe Courteau; 13c Nature PL/Ingo Arndt; 13br Ardea/Jean-Paul Ferrero; 14tr Getty/Berndt Fischer; 14bl Ardea/Mike Watson; 15t Corbis/
Gerolf Kalt; 16tr Seapics; 16bl FLPA/Minden Pictures; 20c Shutterstock/Sarawut Kundej; 20-21 Oceanwide Images/Gary Bell; 20bl Nature PL/Jeff Rotman; 21tc FLPA/Kelvin
Aitken; 21b FLPA; 22br Seapics; 23 Getty/Digital Vision; 23cr Photolibrary/Frank Schneidermeyer; 23c Getty/Visuals Unlimited/Joe McDonald; 24tl Alamy; 24tr Nature
PL/Daniel Gomez; 24bl PA/AP; 24-25 c and l SPL/Paul Whitten; 26 Ardea/Kathie Atkinson; 27tr FLPA/Minden Pictures; 27cr FLPA/Minden Pictures; 27b FLPA/Minden
Pictures; 28tl Getty; 28tl FLPA/Minden Pictures; 28tr FLPA/Minden Pictures; 28br FLPA; 29tr Corbis/Wolfgang Kaehler; 29b NHPA/Daniel Heuclin; 30tr Nature PL/Anup Shah;
30 FLPA/Fritz Polking; 32cl Flickr/vil.sandi; 32br Getty/John Downer; 33bl FLPA/Minden Pictures; 34cr FLPA/Minden Pictures; 34-35 Nature PL/Daniel Heuclin; 35cr SPL/
David T. Roberts; 35b Corbis/Mark Baker; 36c FLPA/Minden Pictures; 37 Animals/Animals/Roger de la Harpe; 36-37 Corbis/Wayne Lynch/All Canada Photos; 38tr Corbis/
Robert Patrick; 38cl Flickr/CDC; 38b SPL/Eye of Science; 39tr SPL/David Scharf; 40tr Nature PL/Martin Dohrn; 40c Nature PL/Martin Dohrn; 41tl FLPA/Minden Pictures;
41tc FLPA/Minden Pictures; 42tr SPL/Roger Harris; 48tl Corbis/Ferdaus Shamim; 48tr Alamy/Adrian Sharratt; 48cr Nature PL/John Downer.

CONTENTS

PREDATOR – *an animal that kills and eats other animals*

KILL OR BE KILLED

In the struggle to survive, many animals have become killer creatures, attacking to defend themselves or to satisfy their hunger. Some are solitary hunters, while others co-operate in packs or even armies. Few corners of the earth – in the air, in water or on land – are safe from predators.

Sharks

A great white lives up to its nickname, 'Jaws', as it grabs a mouthful of tuna. The great white is the ultimate ocean predator. Like other killer sharks, it relies on its senses, speed and terrifying power to locate and overwhelm seals and other prey.

- **Location: almost all oceans**
- **Habitat: coastal waters**
- **Length: 6m**

Big cats

A bloodied Bengal tiger reveals its fearsome fangs. Tigers, lions and other big cats use stealth, speed and sheer power to bring down prey, such as deer.

- **Location: southern Asia**
- **Habitat: rainforest, forests and grasslands**
- **Length: 3m**

Raptors

A harpy eagle makes off with a howler monkey. Eagles, hawks and falcons are the killers of the bird world. Known as raptors, they use their talons to stab prey and their beaks to rip apart flesh.

- **Location: North and South America**
- **Habitat: lowland rainforest**
- **Wingspan: 2m**

 A harpy eagle is armed with super-sharp talons that are up to 13cm long – almost as long as a grizzly bear's claws.

Wolves

A grey wolf tears into a kill. Like African wild dogs and hyenas, wolves hunt in packs, using teamwork, stamina and speed to track prey.

- Location: North America and Eurasia
- Habitat: mountains, forests and tundra
- Length: 1.5m

Amphibians

The brightly coloured skin of the golden poison-dart frog warns of toxins that can kill in seconds. The poison is a defence against predators.

- Location: Colombia, South America
- Habitat: rainforest
- Length: 5cm

Spiders

A Sydney funnel web spider prepares to strike. Efficient killers, spiders inject venom through their fangs to paralyze or kill prey.

- Location: eastern Australia
- Habitat: forested uplands
- Body length: 3.5cm

Snakes

As a gaboon viper bites into a mouse, venom pumps out of its fangs. Not all snakes use venom to kill. Constrictors coil their body around their victim, hugging it to death.

- Location: sub-Saharan Africa
- Habitat: rainforest and savannah
- Length: 1.5m

http://video.nationalgeographic.com/video/worlds-deadliest

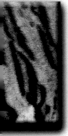

▽ BIG CAT – any large, carnivorous wild animal related to the domestic cat

BIG CATS

Long claws, dagger-like teeth and powerful, crushing jaws – big cats have plenty of weapons. Add to these their sharp senses, stealth, speed and power and you have one of the animal world's top killers. Most big cats are lone hunters, stalking their prey slowly and silently, then sprinting forwards to pounce and deliver the killer bite.

A lioness closes in on a young kudu antelope.

Climbing cats

Leopards drag antelope and other kills up trees, out of the way of scavengers. Like all big cats, leopards use their fang-like canines to grasp a victim around the throat, choking it to death.

Teamwork

The lion is the only big cat that lives and hunts in groups. Fleet-footed lionesses do most of the hunting. Step by step, they approach their prey – a herd of antelope, wildebeest or zebra. Suddenly, one lioness breaks cover to make a kill while the others lend support from the side.

 ❯ If a lion cub is attacked and killed, its mother will eat the corpse.

Killer jaws

Cats use their jagged carnassial teeth, which slice against one another like scissors, to cut up their kill. Small front teeth called incisors nibble flesh from the bone.

A feeding tiger defends its kill.

http://animal.discovery.com/guides/atoz/bcats.html

Living in a pride

Hunting together allows lions to bring down larger prey, providing food for the whole pride. The males protect the kill from hungry scavengers, giving the cubs more time to eat their fill.

"So have I heard on
Africa's burning shore,
A hungry lion give a grievous roar."

William Barnes Rhodes (1772–1826)
from the opera Bombastes Furioso, *1810*

⊖ DEADLY SPRINTER

A cheetah, the fastest animal on land, accelerates faster than most cars, reaching a top speed of 95km/h in 3–4 seconds. Unlike the other big cats, a cheetah cannot retract, or pull back, its claws inside its paws. Instead, the claws work like the spikes on a sprinter's shoes, helping the cheetah to grip the ground. The life-or-death chase across the grasslands is usually over in 20 seconds.

lightweight body with long, thin and muscular legs

Flexible spine powers huge bounds of up to 7m.

Night vision

Most cats hunt at night. At the back of their eyes is a golden layer, the tapetum, which shines when caught in a light. It helps the eyes to absorb extra light, boosting the cat's night vision.

WOLVES OF THE TAIGA

Wolves live and hunt in a pack, up to 30 animals strong. As soon as the pack detects prey – perhaps a herd of caribou or elk – it gives chase, zoning in on any animal that lags behind. Sharp teeth snap at the victim's heels, slowing it down so that other pack members can get a grip. When prey is brought down, the wolves rip at its flesh. For large victims, such as elk, death is often slow.

Feeding time

Wolf packs share their food but there is a strict pecking order. First to feed are the pack leaders – the alpha male and female. Once they give the signal, the rest of the pack can join in. The wolves devour the kill, crushing bones to reach the rich, fatty marrow and leaving little waste.

Wolves are intelligent animals and use calls and physical gestures to communicate with one another.

prey animal

Low head, low ears, low tail – this wolf is under pressure!

Eyes give sharp, binocular vision.

2.5cm-long canines grasp and rip prey.

 > A wolf needs an average of 1.5kg of meat a day. A large kill such as a bison will last a pack of wolves a week.

Bear trouble

Grey wolves in Alaska, USA, attempt to defend their kill from a hungry grizzly bear. Wolves and bears make uneasy neighbours. Bears are big and dangerous but wolf packs can snatch and kill young bear cubs.

⊖ STAMINA AND SPEED

Wolves are muscular and, during a chase, can reach a top speed of 56km/h. At other times, wolves prefer to trot, their long, strong legs covering a metre with each and every stride. They can keep up this pace for hours, covering 100km in a single night.

Each wolf runs in the footprints made by the leader.

Large front feet help to prevent a wolf from sinking in soft snow.

Long hair makes the wolf look larger.

"The aim of life was meat. Life itself was meat. Life lived on life. There were the eaters and the eaten. The law was:
EAT OR BE EATEN."

Jack London (1876–1916)
from the novel White Fang, *1906*

Sensitive ears hear prey up to 16km away.

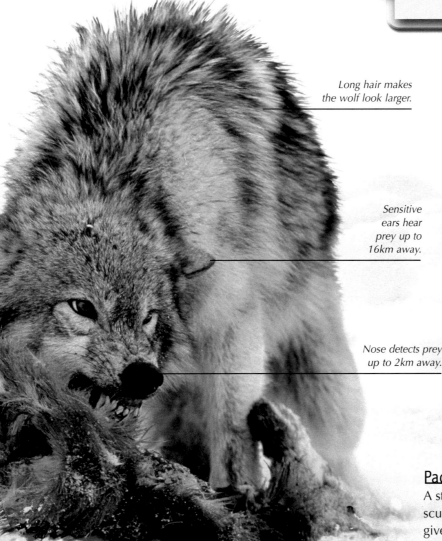

Nose detects prey up to 2km away.

Pack discipline

A strict social order in the pack prevents scuffles from escalating into fights. Youngsters give way to older animals and the weak submit to the strong. All pups develop strength and hunting skills through play fights such as these.

ARCTIC GIANTS

cross-section through hair, shown 350 times bigger than life size

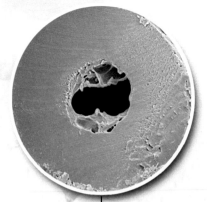

"Something in the bear's presence made [Lyra] feel close to coldness, danger, brutal power..."

Philip Pullman (born 1946)
from the novel Northern Lights, 1995

The largest of all land carnivores, polar bears are also at home in the sea, where their size, power and swimming ability allow them to catch walruses and whales. More commonly, the bears hunt ringed seals at their breathing holes. When a bear senses an approaching seal, it punches the ice with its paw, grabs the seal's head in its jaws and yanks the body on to the ice.

Long outer hairs are hollow, which traps warm air close to the bear's body.

Bear legs

On thin ice, the polar bear's massive feet help to spread its weight over a large area. In water, the paws act as paddles. Polar bears swim with their front legs, stretching out their back legs to work as a rudder.

Learning to hunt

After killing a seal, a polar bear rips open the carcass and, with her cub, feeds on the meat and blubber. Later, the bears will roll in the snow to clean their coats of blood. Females teach their cubs the art of stalking seals, but many attempts fail as the cubs fidget and give the game away.

Out at sea

Polar bears are supreme swimmers and have been seen 100km from land, still powering through the water. In pursuit of prey, they can dive as deep as 4.5m and stay below the surface for more than a minute.

 A large male polar bear on its hind feet stands over 3m tall and weighs more than nine men.

Big, brown bear

Grizzly bears are found in the frozen regions of Russia and North America. These formidable hunters kill prey as large as moose but also catch fish and dig out burrowing creatures, such as ground squirrels.

Strong jaws and a variety of teeth allow grizzlies to feed on any food.

The powerful front paws are equipped with claws up to 15cm long.

Beluga whale's tail thrashes wildly.

short, curved claws for grabbing prey,

white beluga whale, a rare catch for a polar bear

www.polarbearsinternational.org

⊖ NOSY NEIGHBOUR

Polar bears are not usually man-eaters, but hungry ones can pose a dangerous threat. A television cameraman once came face to face with a bear through the window of his cabin. He fired a flare gun to scare it off, but the bear came back – twice. On nights like that it must be hard to sleep!

Feet pads (and nose) are the only furless body parts.

PACK – a troop of animals hunting together

⊜ CRUSHING JAWS

Hyenas have massive jaws filled with strong teeth. Their sharp canine teeth tear at a victim's skin, while the molars are so powerful that they can chew through a zebra's thigh bone to reach the tasty marrow inside.

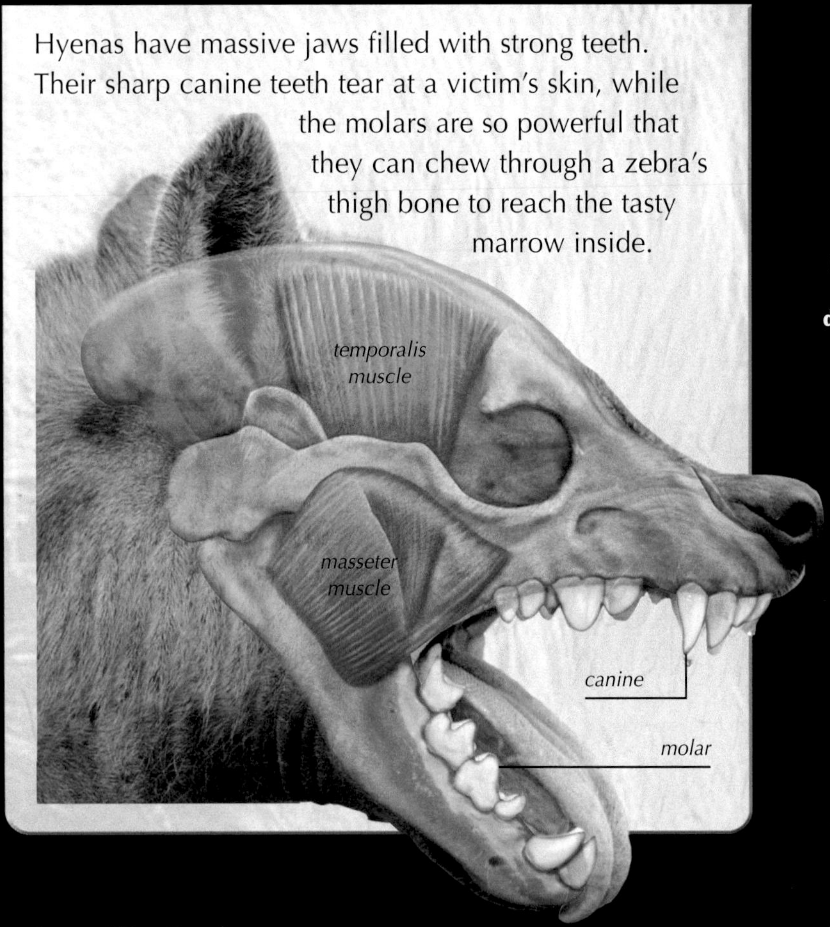

temporalis muscle

masseter muscle

canine

molar

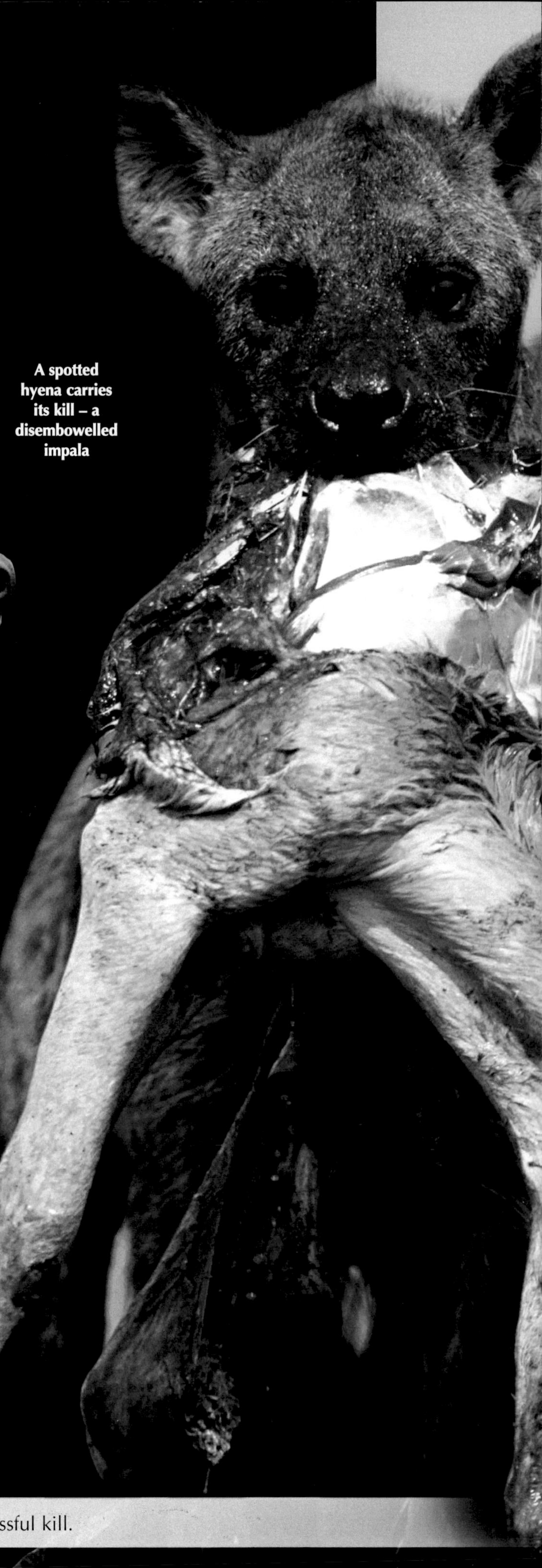

A spotted hyena carries its kill – a disembowelled impala

PACK HUNTERS

Hyenas hunt in packs, which helps them to bring down large prey such as antelope and zebra. These fearless, fast and lightly-built hunters pursue their prey over long distances, taking turns to lead the pack so no individual gets too tired. Other pack hunters include Australian dingoes and African wild dogs.

> Four out of every five attacks by African wild dogs ends in a successful kill.

African wild dog

A female spotted hyena faces up to a pair of snarling African wild dogs.

Bad neighbours

Both hyenas and wild dogs live on the savannah grasslands of Africa. Packs of hyenas will charge wild dogs in an attempt to steal their feast. Who wins will depend on speed, aggression and the number of animals in each pack.

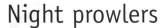

Night prowlers

The hyena looks like a dog but belongs to a different animal family. Hyenas are efficient scavengers and skilful predators. They hunt by night in small groups, killing much larger prey. With strong jaws and powerful digestive systems, they can eat and extract goodness even from their victims' teeth and bones.

Dog meat

Once an animal has been caught by a pack of wild dogs, it is ripped apart. The dogs bolt down their kill before hyenas, lions and vultures move in to pick at the remains.

Dingoes kill kangaroos, wallabies and smaller prey, such as this monitor lizard.

"Hyenas are larger and stronger, but wild dogs attack in formation, like a crack squad of commandos."

Steve Leonard (born 1972)
British wildlife presenter and writer

Wild dog down under

Australian dingoes are descended from wolf-like dogs. They have been known to attack children, so in dingo country parents need to be aware of this danger.

PREDATORY – killing and feeding on other animals

PREDATORY PIRANHAS

Piranhas are small freshwater fish that live in the rivers of South America. They have strong, upturned jaws like those of a bulldog, and remarkably sharp teeth. Not all species of piranha are aggressive, but those that are have a fearsome reputation. When they are hungry and gang up in a school, they work together as one ferocious killing machine, targeting birds, rodents, frogs and young caimans.

Caught by a caiman
A shoal of 20–30 piranhas may be a threat to a young caiman, but this lone fish stands no chance against a fully grown black caiman.

An excited piranha turns on another. Even though these fish hunt together, within the shoal it is every fish for itself.

😐 KILLER JAWS

A piranha's upper and lower teeth fit together so neatly that they can remove a perfect, crescent-shaped chunk of flesh. Amazonian Indians have used the razor-sharp teeth for sharpening darts, shaving and cutting.

In the dry season, piranhas can be stranded in small lakes with little food. This makes them more aggressive.

jaw packed with triangular teeth

> In Brazil about 1,200 cattle are killed by piranhas every year.

Feeding frenzy

A young heron has fallen from its treetop nest into the river. Within seconds, its struggles have alerted a shoal of red-bellied piranhas. Smaller fish size up the prey, taking a few test bites before larger piranhas drag the bird below the surface.

http://library.thinkquest.org/5053/SouthAmerica/piranha.html

Nostrils can detect a single drop of blood in 200 litres of water.

SAVAGE SHARKS

If any animal has the reputation of 'killer creature', it is the shark. Sleek and efficient predators with tiptop senses and massive jaws, sharks hunt prey as large as elephant seals and squid. Some sharks circle their prey and disable it before killing. Others attack by surprise from below.

"What we are dealing with here is a perfect engine, an eating machine."

Matt Hooper
fictional marine biologist in the film Jaws, 1975

Man-eater?

A survivor of a great white shark attack displays his stitches. Great whites are more feared than any other creature in the sea – and with good reason. They carry out more attacks than any other kind of shark.

skin pore

Shark senses

Sharks use many senses to find their prey. They detect vibrations (movement) and even faint trails of blood from wounded creatures. They also sense the weak electrical signals given out by all living things.

The ampullae of Lorenzini are sense organs on a shark's snout that detect electrical signals.

scalloped hammerhead shark

sea lion

> In 2006, there were 62 unprovoked shark attacks on humans.

Gills take in oxygen from the water.

TEETH

A shark's jaws are lined with rows of teeth. Some species have long, narrow, needle-like teeth for impaling fish and other small prey. Those that feed on larger animals have broad, serrated teeth to tear off chunks of flesh. Like disposable razor blades, shark teeth have a short life and are replaced as they break or wear out.

serrated edge for cutting

muscular tail fin

gall bladder

stomach

streamlined body

Large liver helps shark to float.

Strength and speed

A great white smashes into its prey at around 48km/h. In the split second before the impact, it lifts its snout and leads with its upper jaws. The force of the attack carries the shark out of the water with 100kg of meat in its mouth.

FEROCIOUS ORCAS

ORCA – a large, predatory member of the dolphin family, also known as a killer whale

Orcas, also known as killer whales, are giants of the sea. These mammals, which are a type of dolphin, grow up to 9m long and live in family groups called pods. Fast, fierce and intelligent hunters, orcas work together to kill prey very much bigger than themselves, such as great white sharks and humpback whales, as well as hundreds of smaller species.

Athletes of the sea
Killer whales are remarkably agile for their size. They chase and catch fast-moving penguins and fish, and even snap ducks out of the air. They toss their victims out of the water before swallowing them whole.

Sound hunters
Killer whales use a hunting technique called echolocation, which is especially useful in deep, murky water. They send out a stream of high-pitched clicks, then listen for the echoes that bounce back off their prey.

On the shore, sea lion pups are vulnerable and slow.

> There is no known instance of a wild orca killing a person.

www.seaworld.org/animal-info/info-books/killer-whale/habitat-&-distribution.htm

Beach raider

A killer whale surfs on to a beach, where sea lion pups are playing on the shore. It seizes a pup in its huge jaws, then flops back into the water to be washed out to sea. This is a tricky manoeuvre, but the reward of sea lion meat is worth the risk of getting stranded.

> "If they'd wanted to they could have tossed me and my kayak high into the air with just a flick of their tail."
>
> **Steve Leonard (born 1972)**
> *British wildlife presenter and writer*

Orca zooms in at up to 60km/h.

An orca hunts sea lion pups off the coast of Patagonia, Argentina.

☻ MASTER HUNTERS

Killer whales are inventive hunters. As well as using echolocation to find prey, they also make use of other techniques, including herding and trapping. They employ different methods for different types of prey.

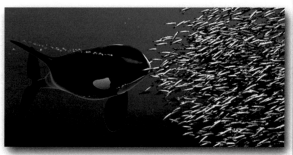

Orcas herd shoals of herring into a tight ball, then slap them with their powerful tails to stun individuals.

After separating a whale calf from its mother, three orcas block off its route up to the surface to breathe.

While staking out a seal hidden in an underwater cave, these orcas hunt and breathe in relay.

Orcas head-butt ice floes to tip off penguins and seals, or whip up the water with their tails to wash them off.

∨ CORAL REEF – *a limestone ridge in shallow, tropical sea water that teems with life*

STINGERS IN THE SEA

In the warm, clear waters off northern Australia lies the Great Barrier Reef, the world's largest system of coral reefs. Built by the skeletons of tiny coral polyps, it stretches for more than 2,000km. The reef supports an astonishing variety of life, including more than 400 different corals. But, divers beware! Lurking in these blue waters are some of the deadliest creatures in the sea.

"In Australia, jellyfish season kicks off in November... Swarms of 3,500–4,000 jellyfish are not uncommon."

Steve Leonard (born 1972)
British wildlife presenter and writer

Blue-ringed octopus

With a body just the size of a golf ball, the blue-ringed octopus contains enough poison to kill ten people. The danger lies in the bite from its parrot-like beak, which is sharp enough to pierce a diver's wetsuit.

⊖ DEATH BY STINGRAY

Stingrays have venomous spines on the end of their tails for protection. Steve Irwin, the Australian conservationist, was killed in 2006 when a stingray whipped its tail barb into his chest and damaged his heart.

diver with southern stingray

 > The largest stingrays are 1.8m wide and 4.2m long, including their tail.

Box jellyfish

The box jellyfish trails a mass of tentacles, packed with stinging cells called nematocysts. Swimmers are easily stung. The pain is excruciating and, without antivenin, a victim can die in just four minutes.

Made up of 95 per cent water, the box jellyfish is almost invisible.

Microscopic, touch-sensitive hairs at the end of each spine trigger the release of poison.

Stonefish

The stonefish is the world's most poisonous fish. It lies quietly on the coral, perfectly camouflaged. A slow mover, it needs a defence: 13 spines along its back that release a deadly poison when touched.

Each tentacle carries millions of stinging cells. Called nematocysts, they have microscopic stinging threads that explode on contact with prey.

http://animals.nationalgeographic.com/animals/invertebrates/common-octopus.html

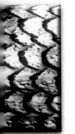

Scary senses

A snake can sense vibrations through the ground, alerting it to nearby prey. It also picks up scents with its tongue. The tongue wipes airborne particles on to the roof of the mouth, where special cells send messages to the snake's brain that allow it to identify the scent.

Diamondback rattlesnake is named for its diamond-shaped markings.

Tail rattle makes sound to warn off predators.

VENOMOUS SNAKES

With its slithering body and lightning speed, the snake is one of the most feared hunters. Many venomous snakes lie in wait for prey. When a victim comes near, the snake rears up and strikes, injecting lethal venom from its fangs. Venom is a clever means of attack, hijacking dangerous prey with little physical contact. The poison paralyzes or kills quickly, and may even begin to break down the body for digestion.

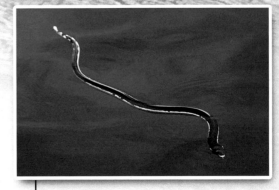

Sea snakes

Found in tropical waters, sea snakes are among the most poisonous reptiles. Luckily, they rarely come into contact with people and are not aggressive. One exception is the beaked sea snake of Australia. It carries out 90 per cent of fatal sea snake attacks.

 > Australia is home to 11 of the top 12 most venomous land snakes.

www.rattlesnakes.com

Spraying venom

As well as injecting prey, a cobra spits venom to defend itself. It can hit an enemy's eyes from as far away as 2.4m, causing temporary blindness.

☻ CAMOUFLAGED KILLERS

With no limbs, many snakes cannot chase prey. Instead, they wait for prey to come to them. They have such excellent camouflage that they are almost impossible to see, especially as they keep so still. Depending on their habitat, snakes have colours and markings that blend in with leaves, vines, sand or rock.

A gaboon viper's markings resemble leaf litter.

Snake detects smells with its nostrils, as well as with the cells of the Jacobson's organ in the mouth.

Venom

Special glands produce the venom, which is squeezed along tiny tubes into the hollow fangs. The venom is forced through tiny openings in the fangs and injected into puncture wounds made by the sharp fang tips.

Forked tongue collects scent particles from the air as it flicks to and fro.

collared lizard

"When you see a rattlesnake poised to strike you, do not wait until he has struck before you crush him."

Franklin D. Roosevelt (1882–1945)
US President, 1933–1945

CONSTRICTOR CRUSH

Constrictors, such as boas, pythons and anacondas, kill with power not poison. When these snakes strike, they rapidly throw muscular coils around their prey's body. Each time the victim breathes out, the coils tighten a little more, so that it cannot breathe in. The tight squeeze also stops the prey's blood flowing. Unable to pump blood, the heart comes to a fatal standstill.

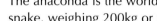

South American giant
The anaconda is the world's heaviest snake, weighing 200kg or more. It lives in or near water, catching capybaras and other animals that come to drink, as well as river turtles and caimans.

young red-tail boa constricting a mouse

A mouse's fate
While suffocating its prey, a boa constrictor keeps a firm grip with sharp, hooked teeth. These teeth are no use for chewing, though, so the boa must swallow its victim whole.

😣 EXPLODING PYTHON

In 2005, in Everglades National Park in Florida, USA, the remains of an alligator were found sticking out of a dead Burmese python. The snake's stomach had been ripped open by the alligator's claws.

| alligator's tail | burst stomach | python's tail |

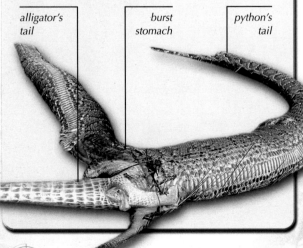

 > The reticulated python is the world's longest snake. It can grow up to 9m long.

Backwards-facing teeth drag in food.

breathing tube

jaws joined by stretchy ligaments

Stretchy jaws

A snake's jaws are joined by ligaments that stretch to give it the necessary gape to eat its super-sized meals. The snake can breathe with its mouth full because it has a movable breathing tube at the front of the lower jaw.

Constrictor's ribs can move apart to make room for swallowed prey.

"None of them knew the limits of [Kaa the python's] power, none of them could look him in the face, and none had ever come alive out of his hug."

Rudyard Kipling (1865–1936)
from the novel The Jungle Book, 1894

Down in one

A boa usually swallows prey headfirst, so the legs do not get stuck in its throat. The snake coats its dinner with slippery saliva, then uses strong muscles to push the food into its stomach. Here, powerful juices dissolve the flesh and bones.

http://animals.nationalgeographic.com/animals/reptiles/boa-constrictor.html

DANGEROUS AMPHIBIANS

The world's most poisonous animal is a small amphibian from the rainforests of Colombia. To deter predators, the golden poison-dart frog has deadly toxins in its skin that attack the nervous system, rapidly causing heart failure. The cane toad is another amphibian that produces poisons in its skin for self defence.

Poisonous toad

The cane toad, a native of Central and South America, is seriously poisonous. Glands on its shoulders produce a milky poison, containing a deadly cocktail of 14 chemicals that cause convulsions and death. Introduced into Australia in the 1930s to control insect pests, the 2-kg toad is now poisoning rare native species.

reservoir of milky poison

Poison glands lie under the warty skin.

Rodent is devoured headfirst by the hungry toad, whose diet also includes insects and small reptiles.

> Poison-dart frogs get their name because the Chocó people of Central America rub the poison on the darts they use for hunting.

http://nationalzoo.si.edu/Animals/Amazonia/Facts/Fact-poisondartfrog.cfm

Ant's body contains poisons – if a frog preys on the ant, the poisons transfer to the frog.

Deadly diet

A poison-dart frog's poison comes from its diet of ants, termites, beetles and centipedes. These minibeasts absorb poisonous chemicals from the plants they eat. Frogs that are moved to a zoo lose their toxicity because they are not eating their natural diet.

Cane toads hunt at night. They locate prey by noticing movement or by tracking their scent.

Colour code

In daylight hours this poison-dart frog is protected by its colours and pattern, which warn other animals that it is best left alone. After dark, predators such as this tarantula are warned off by the taste of the frog's skin.

green poison-dart frog and tarantula

golden poison-dart frog

"Even crocodiles have been found dead with cane toads in their mouths."

Mary Summerill (born 1958)
Presenter of the BBC documentary series Wild Down Under, 2003

⊖ HOW TOXIC ARE THEY?

A golden poison-dart frog is just 5cm long, but its body contains enough poison to kill 10 humans – or an astonishing 25,000 mice. How does that compare with other poisonous creatures?

Golden poison-dart frog could kill 25,000 mice.

Black widow spider could kill 700 mice.

King cobra could kill 3,500 mice.

LIZARD – *a kind of reptile with four legs, a tail and scaly skin*

The Komodo uses its tongue to sniff out potential meals.

Saliva contains more than 60 types of bacteria.

A Komodo can weigh up to 200kg – more than two grown men.

Deadly saliva

Komodo dragons produce saliva full of harmful bacteria, which works as a primitive venom. If prey is wounded but manages to escape, it will die from the infected wound, and the dragon will find and eat it.

LETHAL LIZARDS

Most lizards are carnivorous, but two species have serious bites that can be dangerous to humans. One is the Gila (pronounced 'heela') monster, which lives in deserts in Mexico and southwestern USA. The other is a huge monitor lizard, the Komodo dragon, whose mouth is full of deadly bacteria. The world's largest lizard, it lives on four islands in Indonesia.

⊜ FATAL ATTACK

Tragically, in 2007 a Komodo killed an eight-year-old boy. The animal mauled and bit the child, shaking him viciously from side to side. His family drove off the dragon but the boy died from massive bleeding.

thick, strong neck

scaly, leathery hide

powerful limbs

> The Komodo dragon can detect a potential meal from 5km away, using its flicking tongue to sniff the air.

Scary monster

The Gila monster is a slow-moving lizard. It tries to avoid confrontation if it can by hissing at any animals that challenge it. As a last resort, the Gila will bite, chewing to activate glands in its jaw to produce a poisonous saliva. The toxins, which flow in through the wound, cause paralysis. The Gila's eye-catching colour and skin patterns warn enemies that it is poisonous.

Dinner for six

Six Komodo dragons devour a goat. Komodos move swiftly for their size, and attack water buffaloes, boars and deer. They pin down and rip apart prey with their massive claws. Unfussy diners, Komodos eat carrion, too.

Bead-like, scaly skin is black with pink and yellow markings.

Baby rats are attacked by a Gila monster.

"The breath is very fetid and its odour can be detected at some little distance."

***Scientific American* magazine, 1890**

KILLER CROCODILIANS

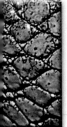

CROCODILIAN – *a member of a group of reptiles that includes crocodiles, alligators and gharials*

They look like prehistoric beasts, but crocodiles and alligators are very much alive, lurking in rivers and lakes. These reptiles are found in subtropical and tropical parts of the world, where the sun warms their cold-blooded bodies and turns them into agile hunters. The saltwater crocodile can grow as long as 5m. It devours fish, other crocodiles, birds, mammals – and unlucky humans.

Big snapper
The gharial nimbly catches fish by sweeping the water with its long, narrow snout. Its needle-like teeth are perfect for spearing slippery prey.

Deadly grip

A Nile crocodile clamps its jaws around a gazelle's neck in a Kenyan game park. Prey this large is a challenge for crocodiles because they cannot chew. They have to spin a kill until it breaks apart.

> Crocodiles and alligators are believed to kill about 2,000 people every year.

Nostril is set high on the skull, so that the crocodile can breathe when hiding in water.

Leathery skin is reinforced with bony, armoured plates called scutes.

New teeth for old

Crocodiles have around 60 teeth. They are designed for grabbing prey rather than cutting flesh. So, to help break down large chunks of meat, crocodilians swallow stones. These churn around in one part of their stomach, grinding up the food.

"Don't think there are no crocodiles because the water is calm."

Malayan proverb

⊖ SHOCK ATTACK

A crocodile's eyes, ears and nostrils are on the top of its head, allowing it to lie low in the water and still see, hear, smell and breathe. To save energy crocodiles wait, motionless, until a meal approaches...

Resembling a log in the river, this Nile crocodile is unseen by its prey – a zebra on its way down to drink.

The crocodile explodes out of the water in a lethal burst, clamping its jaws around the zebra's muzzle.

The terrified zebra slips on the muddy riverbank. Unable to struggle free, it is dragged into deeper water.

The crocodile spins the victim, drowning it or smashing its spine, then breaking the body into chunks.

www.flmnh.ufl.edu/cnhc

Red howler monkeys leap around and call frantically to one another in panic.

Canopy hides sloths, lizards, rodents, birds and many other types of prey.

RAPTOR – a bird of prey, such as an eagle, hawk or falcon

⊖ SILENT HUNTER

Owls hunt at night. Huge eyes help them to see in low light, while their ears alert them to every rustle. The owl's fringed feathers muffle the sound of its wings, so prey rarely hears it coming.

Tengmalm's owl with a mouse

RAPTOR RAID

Eagles, falcons and other raptors have exceptional sight and hearing, plus the speed, strength and lethal talons needed to catch and kill their prey. The birds use different forms of attack. A peregrine falcon drops like a stone to snatch a pigeon in mid-air. A golden eagle flies in low from the side to take its prey by surprise. The still-warm body is carried to a nearby perch, then ripped apart by the powerful beak.

<u>Butcher beak</u>
A golden eagle uses its hooked beak to butcher a hare. Gripping the body with sharp talons, it eats the meat and organs but discards bones and fur. Owls swallow prey whole, but later cough up a neat pellet of bones, feathers or fur.

 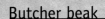 > The peregrine falcon dives at speeds of more than 320km/h, making it the fastest living animal.

Startled scarlet macaws scatter noisily.

Feathered crest is raised during an attack.

Death in the forest

A harpy eagle snatches a red howler monkey from the rainforest canopy, piercing the internal organs with its needle-sharp talons. This skilful hunter manoeuvres itself easily through the dense trees and may be travelling as fast as 80km/h when it dives on its prey.

www.sandiegozoo.org/animalbytes/t-harpy_eagle.html

Curved claws
The talons of this harpy eagle chick will grow up to a formidable 13cm long.

Black widow spider

This female black widow is eating her partner after mating. Despite their name and reputation, however, black widows do not always do this. The female is far more deadly to humans. With venom 15 times deadlier than a rattlesnake's, her bite causes breathing problems and muscle cramps.

Ultra-sensitive hairs pick up sensations from the surrounding area.

"A dark leg quivered in the milk-chocolate earth, then another, and another, until the whole tarantula was revealed."

Nigel Marven (born 1960)
British wildlife presenter and writer

DEADLY ARACHNIDS

Spiders use venom to paralyze or kill their prey. The venom is made in the poison glands, then squeezed along a tube until it shoots out through the spider's fangs. Different venoms work in different ways – some affect muscles and nerves, leading to cramp and paralysis, while others kill tissue around the bite, resulting in scars that are slow to heal. Only about 100 species of spider have venom that is harmful to people.

ARACHNID – *an animal such as a spider or scorpion*

Lifeless male, paralyzed by a bite, is parcelled up in silk.

Super sight
A jumping spider can spy prey from 30cm away, thanks to four pairs of eyes. The two largest eyes move independently, which is why they appear here in different colours.

> The goliath bird-eating spider of South America is the world's largest spider, with a legspan of 26cm.

A female black widow prepares to eat her mate.

◉ SECRET WEAPON

Bird-eating spiders, or tarantulas, can give a painful bite. To attack, they raise the front of the body with legs high in the air, and then strike down using their fangs like pickaxes. Some tarantulas release clouds of hairs from their legs. These have microscopic barbs that stick in the skin – or eye – and are very hard to remove.

On the boat from Brazil

Known for its speed and aggression, the Brazilian wandering spider is one of the world's deadliest spiders. It sometimes turns up in Europe hidden among bananas shipped from Central and South America.

Underside of female's rounded abdomen has red, hourglass-shaped marking.

pedipalp – sensory feeler for tasting food

Dangerous Australian

The Sydney funnel web spider wanders into houses in towns and cities. It bites with fangs strong enough to pierce a fingernail. Victims must find a doctor fast – the venom can kill in under two hours.

STING – *a puncturing organ that can pierce the skin and inject venom*

STING OF THE SCORPION

Scorpions have stung and killed their prey for more than 400 million years – since long before the age of the dinosaurs. These ruthless and efficient hunters often eat their own weight in insects every day, grasping victims with their pincers then using their sting to inject venom. Some scorpions also spray their venom in self defence – it is hideously painful if it enters the eye.

Small but deadly
This deathstalker scorpion's venom is dangerous to people, causing pain, fever, breathing difficulties and even death. When it feels threatened, the 10cm-long deathstalker raises its tail and readies its claws to attack.

Protective poison
A scorpion mother looks after her young. She carries her brood on her back for the first few days of their lives, with her poison-tipped tail curled over them to keep enemies at bay.

scorpion eating a blowfly

⊖ HAIRY HUNTER

The rock scorpion lives in southern Africa. It hides in cracks between the rocks by day, coming out to hunt at dusk. Its fine body hairs can detect vibrations made by any nearby spiders and insects.

"Lord! how we suddenly jump, as Scorpio, or the Scorpion, stings us in the rear."

Stubb
second mate on the Pequod in Herman Melville's Moby Dick, 1851

Sting in the tail

A northern scorpion feeds on a blowfly.
Scorpions range in colour from yellow and tan
to brown and black. Like spiders, they belong
to the arachnid family, but they store venom
not in the fangs but in their muscular tail.
The poison glands and sting are in
the tail's last segment.

Muscles swing the sting into position and rock it to and fro.

Venom is squeezed out of the sting.

Venom is produced in tiny venom sacs.

www.bbc.co.uk/nature/life/scorpion

DISEASE SPREADERS

Some creatures do not mean to kill but, when they feed on other animals, they pass on germs and disease. These creatures harbour parasites – tiny organisms that live, feed and breed inside them. Some mosquitoes, for example, carry a parasite that causes malaria. By spreading it to humans when they bite, these insects kill more people than any other killer creature.

African killer

Tsetse flies feed on the blood of humans and cattle. They spread a parasite that causes a fatal illness called sleeping sickness in humans.

"A vampire bat... needs to drink at least half its bodyweight every night. Collecting that is not easy."

David Attenborough (born 1926)
British broadcaster and naturalist

Fly's eye, with its thousands of surfaces, is superb at detecting movement.

Mosquito

The female anopheles mosquito spreads malaria. Other species of mosquito can spread dengue fever, yellow fever and other dangerous diseases.

Bacteria on legs and mouth cause diarrhoea and dehydration.

Fly spits on its food, then sucks it up through spongy mouthparts.

Common as muck

House flies feed on animal droppings and rotting matter. They carry harmful germs that contaminate food. The infections they cause kill many children in poorer countries of the world.

⊖ MINIATURE KILLERS

Fleas carry deadly diseases such as typhus. In the Middle Ages, millions died of bubonic plague, carried by fleas living on black rats.

Bat attack

Vampire bats drink the blood of sleeping animals. They cut the skin with their sharp front teeth, then lap up the blood. If a bat is carrying the rabies virus, the disease is passed on through the bite. Rabies affects the nervous system and the brain, leading to madness and death.

A bat navigates by echolocation (above). When it nears a victim – such as a sleeping pig – it lands.

The bat makes its final approach on all fours. As it feeds, a substance in its saliva keeps the blood flowing.

KILLER COLONY

COLONY – a large group of animals that live together

Which animals form an army and eat every creature in their path? Army ants, which live in the Americas. They march on a million feet across the jungle floor. Cockroaches, scorpions, tarantulas, crickets – all run for their lives. When an army ant finds its prey, it releases a chemical that 'calls out' to its comrades. In seconds, hundreds of ants arrive to sting the victim, dismember its body and carry it back to the nest.

ANT IN CLOSE-UP

An ant's body has three parts – a head, thorax and abdomen. The head has the mouth, eyes and antennae. The mouth has two scissor-like jaws called mandibles. Army ants are blind and rely on their antennae to smell, touch and communicate.

thorax

head

abdomen

"Go to the ant, you lazybones; consider its ways, and be wise."

Proverbs 6.6, in the Old Testament of the Bible

Ant food

Army ants feed mainly on other insects, but will kill lizards and snakes. Driver ants, which also form colonies but live in Africa, can smother and kill animals as large as chickens, pigs and goats if they are cooped up or tethered.

> A single colony of army ants can kill and eat up to 100,000 insects in a day.

Antbirds perch above the ants, ready to pick off insects fleeing the colony.

Living nests

As army ants move around the forest, they use their own bodies to build temporary night-time nests called bivouacs. The queen and her eggs are safe in the middle of the mass of ants.

In a tangle

Ants use their own bodies to build bridges – for example, linking a bivouac to the ground. The individual ants cling together with their clawed feet.

Large robber fly is ready to snatch any injured insects.

Each ant finds its way by detecting chemicals given off by other ants.

Army on the march

A column of army ants snakes across the leaf litter. At the front of the column, the soldiers fan out, covering an area 10m wide. Prey creatures are stung, then hacked to pieces by the ants' jaws. The army makes thousands of kills a day.

EXTINCT KILLERS

About 100 million years ago, in the swamps of what is now Argentina, there lived a terrifying predator – *Giganotosaurus*. With its huge head, 20cm-long teeth, clawed hands and massive, muscular legs, *Giganotosaurus* probably takes the title as the scariest of all the meat-eating dinosaurs. It was even bigger than its North American cousin, *Tyrannosaurus rex*.

Sail-like structure on back may have been used to regulate body temperature, or for display.

Ferocious theropod

All carnivorous dinosaurs belong to a group that scientists call theropods. *Spinosaurus* was a huge theropod – perhaps as long as 18m – that lived in north Africa 95 million years ago. With its long, crocodilian head, it probably fished rather than hunting on land.

"A single *Giganotosaurus* – even a huge alpha male – is no match for a mature *Argentinosaurus*."

Henry Gee (born 1962)
British palaeontologist

whip-like tail

Following the herd

Giganotosaurus probably lived in small family groups, stalking herds of *Argentinosaurus* and other giant plant-eaters as they moved to new feeding grounds. At 35m long, an adult *Argentinosaurus* was too large to bring down, but small teams of *Giganotosaurus* worked together to pick off younger members of the herd.

Deinonychus foot with outsize claw

Anatomy of a killer

With its long hind legs and light bone structure, *Deinonychus* was a fast sprinter. Each of its feet had one huge, curved claw for hooking into prey.

Argentinosaurus *was a sauropod, a long-necked, plant-eating dinosaur.*

1.8m-long skull, attached to jawbone lined with 20cm-long serrated teeth

☻ PACK HUNTERS

Deinonychus was an intelligent, speedy, wolf-sized predator. It hunted in packs, stalking and ambushing prey. Members of the pack leapt at their victim in a co-ordinated attack, hanging on with hook-like claws as they bit into the flesh. In this way, *Deinonychus* could hunt prey big enough to provide food for several days.

downy feathers for warmth

powerful legs for sprinting

Heavy tail helps to counterbalance the enormous head.

http://www.nhm.ac.uk/jdsml/nature-online/dino-directory/

GLOSSARY

abdomen
In animals such as insects and arachnids, the tail end of the body.

amphibian
A cold-blooded animal that lives on land but breeds in water, for example a frog.

antenna (plural: antennae)
In insects, one of a pair of sensory feelers that stick out from the head.

antivenin
A substance containing antibodies that counteract the effects of animal venom.

bacterium (plural: bacteria)
A simple micro-organism. Some bacteria can cause disease.

binocular vision
Seeing that involves two eyes working together, allowing the viewer to judge distances. The eyes face forwards to give overlapping fields of view.

blubber
The thick layer of fat beneath a sea mammal's skin that keeps its body warm in the extreme cold.

camouflage
The use of colour or pattern to blend in with the surroundings and escape the notice of predators.

canine teeth
Also known as fangs or dogteeth, the four pointed teeth at the front of a mammal's mouth on either side of its incisors, used for gripping meat.

canopy
The highest part of a rainforest, where the trees spread out their branches.

carcass
The dead body of an animal.

carnassial teeth
The large teeth near the back of a carnivore's jaw, used for shearing at flesh and bone.

carnivorous
Describes a flesh-eating animal, especially one from the *Carnivora* order, which includes dogs, cats and bears.

carrion
The flesh of a dead animal.

cold-blooded
Describes an animal that cannot control its own body temperature, which changes according to the surroundings.

disembowelled
Describes a body when its vital organs have been ripped out.

echolocation
The way that some animals, such as bats, find their way and locate prey, by making sounds and using the returned echoes to work out their surroundings.

extinct
Describes an animal or plant that has died out globally, never to reappear.

gland
A group of cells or an organ in the body that produces a particular substance, such as poison.

incisors
A mammal's sharp-edged front teeth.

ligament
Tough, fibrous tissue that connects muscle to bone.

mammal

An animal that gives birth to live young, which feed on mother's milk. Lions and bears are mammals.

mandibles

In insects, mouthparts used for biting and crushing food.

marrow

Fatty, protein-rich tissue that fills the hollow centre of bones.

molars

The broad teeth found at the back of a mammal's jaw, used for grinding food.

nematocyst

A tiny stinging cell that injects venom into prey or an attacker. Jellyfish are armed with nematocysts.

palaeontologist

A scientist who studies the fossils (preserved remains) of extinct animals.

paralysis

A state in which the body – or part of it – loses the ability to move or feel. Venom can cause paralysis and death.

polyp

A tiny aquatic creature with a tube-shaped body. Coral reefs build up from the leftover skeletons of dead polyps.

predator

An animal that hunts and kills other animals.

prey

An animal that is hunted and killed by other animals.

rainforest

A thick forest, with very tall trees, that grows in tropical countries where it is hot all year round and rains every day.

reptile

A cold-blooded animal with scaly skin, for example a snake. Some reptiles lay eggs and others give birth to live young.

saliva

Liquid produced in the mouth to make food easier to swallow.

savannah

An area of grassland and scattered trees, found in tropical or subtropical regions.

scavenger

An animal that feeds on carrion.

subtropical

Found in the subtropics – the warm region between the hot tropics and the cooler, temperate parts of the world.

theropod

A two-legged, carnivorous dinosaur with extremely sharp teeth and claws. All theropods belonged to the saurischian, or lizard-hipped, group of dinosaurs.

thorax

In animals such as insects, the middle part of the body, found between the head and abdomen.

toxin

A poisonous substance, especially one formed in the body.

tropical

Found in the tropics – the hot parts of the world on either side of the Equator.

venom

The poisonous fluid that some animals, such as snakes, inject into their prey.

INDEX

INVESTIGATE

Encounter killer creatures for yourself in zoos, safari parks and museum exhibits, or find out more on the page or onscreen.

lions at a safari park

Zoos and safari parks

Visit a zoo or safari park to get up close to a range of predators, and to find out about breeding programmes and other conservation measures to protect animals in the wild.

Four Corners: Zoos by Bob Barton (Longman)

Chester Zoo, Chester, Cheshire, CH2 1LH, UK

www.safaripark.co.uk

museum exhibit of an animatronic Sydney funnel web spider

Museums and exhibitions

Natural history museums have displays and expert information about all sorts of predators, as well as stuffed specimens and dinosaur fossils. Look out for themed exhibitions, too.

Natural History Museum Book of Predators by Steve Parker (Carlton)

National Museum, Chambers Street, Edinburgh, EH1 1JF, UK

www.museum.manchester.ac.uk/kids/galleries/liveanimals/

golden eagle fitted with a documentary camera

Documentaries and movies

Award-winning documentaries and films allow you to watch predators displaying natural behaviour in their own habitats. Try an up-close IMAX film – if you dare!

Big Cat Diary: Cheetah by Jonathan Scott and Angela Scott (Collins)

IMAX 3D cinema, Science Museum, Exhibition Road, London, SW7 2DD, UK

www.bbc.co.uk/nature/animals/

illustration from Biography of a Grizzly (1900) by Ernest Thompson Seton

Books and magazines

If you enjoy absorbing facts and looking at stunning photographs, check out some of the many information books and magazines about dangerous animals. Your local librarian may also be able to suggest some exciting narrative accounts of predators.

Kingfisher Knowledge: Dangerous Creatures by Angela Wilkes (Kingfisher)

Shell Wildlife Photographer of the Year exhibition, Natural History Museum, Cromwell Road, London, SW7 5BD, UK

www.nationalgeographic.co.uk